# NAZIS, COMMIES, AND TERRORISTS

How western society has become what it fought,
and how to fix this problem

TARL WARWICK

2014

# INTRODUCTION

In our modern world much has been made of the tolerance of the present era- "we are not like people living a century ago, for now we tolerate everyone" they say- but this new-found progressive tolerance has come at a steep cost, and those who most support liberty are ironically those who are most wont to cripple liberty, while those who are the most loving towards this concept of tolerance are also those who do the most to create an atmosphere of intolerance towards views they fear, misunderstand, or personally dislike.

Indeed, the intolerance of far-right nationalism, of racially tinged philosophy, of imperialistic eras long before, hasn't been done away with so much as it has been transformed from a far right intolerance into a far left one; where we mention *far right* and *far left* we have to differentiate between Europe and the Americas, as well as other locations, because what passes for one of these two fringes in one hemisphere often is antithetical in the other; someone who appears to be far to the right of the political and social spectrum in, say, Sweden, would be considered a centrist in the United States, and a liberal here would find themselves considered a "bit far to the right" in the opposite situation.

The current situation in this world is predominantly one of confusion all around- people are beginning to lose their own personal and cultural identity because they are constantly being pitted against one another on the internet and by business and government.

More specifically, what we have seen of late is much like the move from right wing to left wing intolerance- for the same thing is happening with regards to imperialism; those who believe (and they are uniformly self-proclaimed leftists or liberals) that colonialism ended have purposely blinded themselves and planted their head in the sand like an ostrich. Colonialism never ended- the commonwealth of Britain is still very much present, and all French speaking African states remain essentially French vassals through trade- meanwhile the United States has continued to expand its already massive sphere, although in this special case we can say almost every decision and action is taken on the basis of money rather than morality- for the USA will gladly do business with the most tyrannical Arabian dictator if it means business was good.

Russia, too, despite its collapse has maintained vigilance over its sphere. At the time of this writing their own economy appears to be sliding into irrelevance because it relies upon fuels which are soon to be outdated (that is the hope of all civilized peoples, at least) but they retain the one commonality of modern imperial powers, which is that of nuclear weaponry. These same states, in order to stanch any competition out, have attempted to prevent all others from obtaining such weapons, except in cases where it wasn't possible to do so, such as with India and Pakistan, or North Korea, which is a satellite of China and is thus allowed a limited program designed only to intimidate and stave off any South Korean or Japanese militarization.

It is here that we see (merely) the beginning rudiments of the point I'm trying to make, and these are the forerunners of my arguments here, and must be expressed not because they relate to National Socialism, or censorship, or militarization, or anything else related to these, but because they are related intrinsically under the umbrella of oppression; for that is truly the point here; that in our haste to demolish ideologies we found morally reprehensible, we began adopting the same reprehensible views and actions taken by those same groups. In this we may drag in a bit of Nietzsche, and say that perhaps we stared into the abyss too long and it imprinted upon our cultural consciousness.

And it isn't in regards just to the Nazis or Nazi Germany that this has happened- the western world also ended up adopting some of the worst customs of the communists, specifically around the time we most virulently and bitterly competed with them, and our battle-scarred visage of a nation has perhaps been irreparably altered for the worse because of our run-ins with islamofascists in the more modern age. True, some within our political establishment, and some within society itself, oppose such draconian, tyrannical, and dishonest moves, but our steady slide from a liberated people of the west into our eventual future downfall at our own hands because of increasing censorship, domestic militarization, foreign interventionism, and ill-advised and confused quasi-nationalism and quasi-racism is at this point moving from "likely" to "inevitable" and there are those who fear the latter has already been achieved.

# I: THE ROOTS OF EUGENICS AND MODERN RACISM IN THE USA

Before I can even attempt to describe how the Nazis, Soviets, and Islamofascists have indelibly left a stain on our supposedly civilized culture, I must first delve into the roots of the Nazi movement courtesy not only of *The Antediluvian World* and German mysticism in the Thule tradition which informed some of the madness of Himmler (and Hitler, supposedly, although to a lesser and less certain extent) but anthropology and social science, which long before Hitler attained puberty had already begun to discuss the issues of race, colonialism, and ethics with regards to ethicity, nationalism, and sterilization.

It is known, established fact, and widely admitted within anthropological and sociological circles that the rudiments of eugenics first began in the United States-early armchair experts in all social fields had already laid the groundwork for eugenics when scarred, shellshocked men from the fields of the civil war were still in their prime of life. And it was in this state that the western world, which had once been marginally more tolerant of those outside established "civilized" culture gave birth to the confused monstrosity that was later to become European racial nationalism- for nationalism itself had largely been abandoned in favor of confused ideals which were never realistic to begin with, to the point where figures such as Rudolf Steiner, who had written on the concept of tribal blood by the 1910s, was later decried as a Jewish fanatic by the Nazi party- in the modern age, most tolerant leftists would consider him a racist heretic.

I myself studied anthropology at the University of Vermont, and a great deal was said and a great issue made of the birth of eugenics and how the University there was intrinsically connected to it- it was, in fact, a seat of sterilization for Native Americans up until the 1970s, long after eugenics had fallen out of favor with the public. Indeed, segregation had already ended in the most deeply racially charged parts of the former Confederacy, but eugenics lived on in the laboratories and conference rooms of the Yankee North for decades afterward, and would possibly never have ended at all had people not become aware of its abusive nature.

In the age of armchair experts we also saw another facet of social consciousness arise that led to an equally grotesque level of abuse and an equally large or perhaps larger death toll- for Marx was, at the time, heading into old age, having already unleashed upon the world an idealistic but ultimately unworkable communism, delivering it like the injection of a needle into the wanting veins of society. That Marx' notion of primitive communism has been utterly destroyed by modern archaeology and a cursory review of ancient remains alone, not to mention all other evidence, is clear- but it was this age of self proclaimed prophets, philosophers, and revolutionaries that led directly to the confused modern state we find ourselves in.

Marx might be seen as the equally abusive opposite to what had become the general western obsession with categorizing people into hierarchies- not really an opposite however, because the principle of categorization remained the same, and he and others merely applied it to class rather than some heritable condition such as ethnicity or skin tone. To Marx, primitive man as understood by the west was actually an advanced, hedonistic sort of proto-human ape which held all ownership in common at equal levels, such that nobody had ownership over anything other than perhaps a few baubles others in the tribe were unable to use- the principle of collectivism that he saw in ancient man (though now debunked entirely) was simply a more positive stereotype and label he gave them, which was roughly equivalent to the usual European tendency of seeing people in terms of whether they were savages, barbarians, civilized, or advanced. In the American sense, it was important only that the race in consideration be of light complexion and that it was lawful and organized, cutting out the barbarian category altogether.

Slavery has become a great issue as well in hindsight, but most Americans remain blissfully unawares that the majority of slaves were held in Latin America and that the United States held relatively few- and would never have had legally recognized slavery at all had it not been for a man named Anthony Johnson gaining perpetual ownership of a formerly indentured worker. That Johnson was himself black and technically on the culmination of the Casor suit became the first legal slave owner in the 13 Colonies escapes the notice of most. They live under the illusion that slavery was an 1800s era issue involving cotton, ignoring its 17th century roots in the new world.

As time went on the going tendency of supposedly enlightened individuals to see only skin color and hear only an accent grew more and more dominant- the moment the Irish potato famine led to coffin ships full of immigrants landing in New York and elsewhere, populism began expanding rapidly, and people who are now regarded only as white Europeans were temporarily relegated to secondary status. The image of the short, fat, bottle-holding drunken Irish immigrant ranting in an alcohol driven daze and perpetually out of work, or of the large-nosed "Iberian" wench prostituting herself because she wasn't a protestant took hold, and fairly soon groups that would later reconcile spent several decades infighting.

Here we see one of the early examples of the still persistent racial confusion present in the United States especially, but also elsewhere- the term *race* itself has become so utterly malleable, and has been malleable for so long, that it has almost lost any meaning at all. In the 1800s, every "white" American was certain that the Irish were a sort of bastardized sub-race with characteristics deliberately likened to those of Africans from popular culture at the same time- this was done not because of some illusion that they were of similar origin, but rather to show the level of disdain for them was similar (because to "native" white Americans, the Irish were unwelcomed immigrants competing for the same money- and here we see an early example of how money and power has informed American conceptions of race and warped them beyond any proper, pragmatic classification scheme.)

In the modern age most American ethnic and racial animosity has been directed at the newest prevalent group of immigrants available for populist politicians to exploit for their own gain- namely those of Hispanic descent, especially of Mexican nationality. Most of those who fervently decry them as job stealing criminals have never met them, and most of those who support any and all increase in immigration have never studied the impact thereof on certain states' economies. As such, we're left with an impossible scenario, in which those with the most and most self-important opinions of these groups are those least qualified to judge the situation.

To the average "racially conscious" (as though the term meant anything) American, who themselves is a creole of multiple cultures, the immigrants coming across the border are a grave threat- but not because of their (European) language or their (mostly European) social heritage, nor are they concerned with their racial composition, which in most cases is an admixture of the same European and Mesoamerican groups that the average citizen of the United States is comprised of. Rather than focus on these issues, wherein they'd be forced to admit that the Mexican is as white as they are, they instead focus on money and, spurred on by politicians eager to grab some populist votes, they remain ignorant but convinced that somehow these Hispanics are fundamentally different from themselves. This would be the amusing equivalent of a Spanish man and a German man arguing over who was "More European."

And the Hispanics themselves have been just as misled by money grubbing politicians. Convinced that our "liberal" politicians care about anything other than their tax money or votes, they persist in voting for people who are generally, as an aggregate, far older than themselves, far richer than themselves, and who are almost entirely of anglosaxon origin.

That a billionaire from New England with an English ancestral background can somehow convince the Hispanic population that they "understand" their plight is a claim no more convincing than that that same billionaire can sympathize with the plight of the average working class New Englander. And although some of us have been sheltered from the greed and big money of politics by virtue of living in extremely rural areas where the politicians in question are forced to mingle with the general population with regularity, that does not make those same politicians any less out of touch. In the field of race, at least some of the confusion has to be ascribed to its misuse by the wealthy and powerful who, clinging to their corrupt money and power, endeavor always to encourage people to vote along racial lines, ethnic lines, or, more honestly, monetary lines (the last of which will almost never be mentioned in a campaign being run by competent officials except in extremely poor districts, which as before will almost invariably be represented by someone who was born wealthy or who became wealthy.)

To our last point about money's effect upon racial consciousness we need look no further than the election pertaining to Barack Obama and his rival John McCain- for the media constantly reminded the nation of how humble Obama was compared to his opponent, when they were both millionaires. In this context, we were led dishonestly to compare their wealth to one another, rather than compare our own general wealth to either of the candidates, at which point the two candidates became indistinguishable to the average American.

The fact that minority groups voted heavily in favor of Obama, also, was less the result of some sort of racial motivation than that he seemed "more average" to the average person, and of course, like seeks like- the voter, unable to find much similarity between themselves and either candidate, was goaded into comparing the two only on their age and monetary substance, such that a comparison could be drawn- here again I mention anthropology, at least in modernity, and especially in linguistics where it is now a well regarded concept that the human mind understands the world predominantly in terms of opposing forces- and it's inarguable that, for example, a white sheet of paper is more visible against a black background than a background of its own color. Using this principle, the media and political elite have managed to fool the majority of citizens into thinking there is an intrinsic difference in races where the politician's skin color, ethnic background, or monetary views as conceivably applied to race are the only major differences between the two. This concept of opposites is important in considering further issues of race.

## II: HOW THE NAZIS CONQUERED THE WEST

When I claim that the Nazis conquered the Western world some will frown and think that I must have become a lunatic- but it is not only a subjective claim but an objective one, when we begin to observe not only what happened in the United States and elsewhere during the second world war, but shortly thereafter- and it has continued even to the modern day. We are all familiar with the internment camps instituted here in the 1940s, and how Japanese citizens who had done nothing wrong were rounded up in a manner astonishingly similar to that of the Jews in Germany around the same time, with the general excuse that they might be loyal to Japan and commit espionage.

That few if any of these citizens were ever loyal to Japan was already evident shortly after the war ended- in fact the long suffering Japanese who had been so woefully mistreated by our own government hardly raised a peep afterward, and almost immediately re-integrated into the same society they had been forcibly removed from. Similarly, some of German and Italian descent were interned as well, equally without a purpose. The government later apologized for these actions, but at the time they were undertaken, an undercurrent of general panic had set in, and the government reflected this as much as the people began to reflect the will of those in positions of authority.

Here we have to list a few complaints lodged against Nazism at the time by the Western world; we need not bullet the list, and it will suffice to mention only a few-mainly, that they were abusive of mind, body, and soul.

In the first, abusive towards the body, IE: physically attacking, imprisoning, executing, and generally endorsing and carrying out violence towards their own citizenry and towards those of foreign nations which were themselves citizens (read; not actively in combat.)

In the second, abusive towards the mind, IE: The media at the time was censored, state-run, and that ideas considered antithetical to the morality and doctrines seen as appropriate by the Nazi authorities were either frowned upon, suppressed, or violently purged, depending on the degree of disagreement and the degree to which the antithetical views could possibly be seen as advocating any form of overthrow of the Nazi regime.

In the third and final, abusive towards the soul, IE: The Nazi government insinuated itself into situations in which it became the arbiter of people's personal spiritual beliefs. Hitler was regarded as of high importance, and although he alluded to and apparently lauded various deified forces (including his native Catholic god) the cult of personality around him caused even those religious groups which he tolerated to suffer as they argued amongst themselves over whether Hitler being almost deified in such a manner was something they could tolerate. While some bishops reigned over Nazi ceremonies, others were trying to save as many Jews as possible.

The communists were doing essentially the same thing at the same time that the Nazis had been doing. Communism had been attacked in the West, but such attacks went into a hiatus the moment Hitler attacked the Polish.

Here we see a strange disconnect. The holomodor (which to this day some deny) took as many lives, or possibly more lives, as the holocaust did, and was no less organized, no less deadly, and with no fewer death camps dotting the landscape- for the wire fences of Auschwitz merely became the generic concrete slabs of any gulag in which prisoners were kept indefinitely and tortured as they slowly starved or died of exposure. In a few especially insane cases, the slave labor found therein was related to atomic development, and some of these remote caves to this day remain fenced off, to keep the haphazard tourist from accidentally wandering too close to a highly radioactive pit of uranium tailings- the same pit hundreds of workers probably froze to death next to back in the 1950s.

Despite the similarities, the way in which modern culture treats the two- the Nazis and the communists (represented respectively by the atrocities of the holocaust and holomodor)- are widely and vastly separate. The average American, or European, would react with hostility towards someone wearing a shirt emblazoned with a swastika, but replace that hated symbol with a hammer and sickle and they either ignore it or find it amusing.

But these things are all tangential to my point here, for the similarities between action and the resultant disparity between treatment thereafter matter less than the issue at hand, which is merely that *The Nazis, while losing the physical war with the west, won the ideological war, because their most fervent critics adopted their same ideas and strategies.*

The modern day left in Europe has actually imprisoned people for the crime of having National-Socialist, racist, or even strictly nationalist tendencies. This has led to a situation in which those who most dislike and distrust the Nazis have themselves become just like them- because the only method they have to strictly suppress Nazism is to endorse the same type of suppressive strategies that they themselves used to use. In saying this here, I am fully aware that some will assume that this is somehow in defense of the Nazis- a common claim used by those who are dishonest enough not to want valid philosophical argument on the subject; unfortunately, most people eat it right up and don't dare to make the same comparison, however apt it may be, for fear of forever wearing the scarlet letter "A"- not here for adultery but rather for antisemitism.

Rather, I am not comparing Nazis favorably with anyone, but rather the dishonest modern day censorship-happy folks from the "tolerant" left with the Nazis themselves, having been transmuted into that which they had formerly hated with such great tenacity.

The term "Nazi" itself has somewhat been watered down into disuse because of the tendency for it to be dragged out any time someone dislikes the actions of another, indicating their belief that the actions in question are draconian. This semi-humorous use of a formerly taboo term has created a situation in which anyone of a workaholic, or "too strict" nature might be jokingly called a Nazi, or Hitler, or something along those lines.

At the same time, it's clear the average person on the left retains their ability to draw a more intelligent comparison- when the police beat down a civilian they are "Nazis" or at least like them, and a politician seeking ever to absorb more power and grind people down with taxes or regulations is also a Nazi- and although they most certainly, usually, are not members of a white nationalist group, or of an actual dedicated National Socialist party, the comparison here is at least sensible and shows their ability to understand the concept of Nazi as "one who is draconian, evil, and obsessed with work and order."

And here we must insert the very real realization that the kind of policing taking place as we speak- with heavy surveillance and formerly plainclothes officers more and more closely approximating an elite military order- is more and more closely approximating the kind of perpetual domestic military state which existed not only during the era of the Third Reich, but also afterward in Soviet controlled East Germany, which is a good segue into the next section, as it relates to the brutality of yet another regime whose ideologies we copied all over the Western world.

# III: THE USA BECAME THE SAME AS THE USSR

Much like with the Nazis in Germany, the communists running Russia from the era of Lenin all the way up through to the times of collapse of the USSR, were also a surveillance happy bunch, hellbent on weaponizing anything they could- in what might be the funniest development, developed militaries began using trained dolphins to conduct underseas maneuvers related to undersea mines. Famously, we can point to the fantastic movie *Doctor Strangelove* (*"How I Learned to Stop Worrying and Love the Bomb"*) as a sort of representation of the entire cold war period, in which leaps in technological progress were made, but almost always as an accident related to weapons development. In this film, even as the nuclear bombers have been irrevocably sent into flight towards their respective targets, a suggestion is made on the basis of the comments of the doctor (a former Nazi himself) that more mineshafts need to be built to house refugees of the atomic war, and that the communists may have a secret mineshaft program, and that the "mineshaft gap" (a humorous but dark reference to every other facet of the arms race) must be closed. In what may be a reference to the Nazi-era roots of weaponization which could destroy the world, used over petty differences in ideology, the movie closes with the doctor, formerly wheelchair bound, standing up and shouting *"Mein Furher... I can walk!"* Subsequently, the entire world is presumably annihilated, and footage of nuclear weapons exploding is set to Vera Lynn's "We'll Meet Again"- although it's not clear in such a scenario that any survivors would meet anything but smoking corpses dusted with radioactive ash.

During the cold war the United States and the entirety of western Europe, still under capitalism, learned quickly from the same Nazi scientists and propagandists who had been absorbed during Operation Paperclip- an attempt to secure as much Nazi technology and as many of its professionals as possible, specifically to give the west a technological advantage over the Soviet Union. The operation was a complete success, and although the Soviets gained access to East Germany, the bulk of the elite science of Nazism was grabbed up by the USA and by the British, as the Germans fled towards western lines, specifically to prevent themselves from suffering a worse fate at the hands of the Russians, who sought collective punishment on all German people, including civilians who had already seen their nation burn- that at the end of the war the allies endorsed saturation bombing and crushed Dresden and other cities in still-debated bombing runs designed only to kill mass numbers of civilians is clear, and some (legitimate) criticism of the west has also been made on the subject of nuclear weapons being deployed on an already largely defeated Japanese mainland- targeting cities which were mostly civilian areas, killing upwards of 150,000 people in just two atomic drops.

Thus, the west not only began to adopt the surveillance and militarism of the same foes it defeated and later the same communists they opposed, but also quite literally absorbed the great thinkers so-called of the former, adapting technology and military goods that had been developed by Nazis, sometimes as the result of human experimentation and torture.

General Patton wanted to reorganize and launch an offensive on the Soviets before they had the chance to recover from having had their entire western front decimated by the Nazis during bitter fighting- had he gotten his wish it's conceivable that communism would have died shortly after Nazism did, and our own government may never have gotten the moral go-ahead to build the sorts of weapons we now possess, which wouldn't have been needed had there not been a Soviet Union to hold an arms race with, for by this time the United States, having armed itself, already possessed a quantitative and qualitative military superiority that put it well beyond the capability of any other nation to assault. Patton was denied his wish, and the reason for this is still possibly speculative.

The United States began to look a lot like the same communists it opposed; surveillance expanded greatly, and Hoover era "gangs and Tommy guns" romanticism gave way to the shadowy espionage of men in gray coats in unmarked vehicles tapping people's phones to determine if they were loyal. Nobody was safe from the espionage, and propaganda was everywhere- and yet the entire time this was happening, the American people were reminded that somehow this was different from the same thing that was happening in the Soviet lands to the east- because somehow surveillance here was "not the same" as surveillance there. Labeling all opposition as unpatriotic and possibly communist, the government gained free reign to abuse its power whenever possible, even while they admittedly carried out experiments on the general population in defiance of our constitutional protections.

The tendency of a government to ignore its own legal constraints and go ahead with the most draconian measures it can get away with is understood to be more or less universal; "Power corrupts" they all say, and yet when they regard our own government using the same methods that the communists or Nazis once did, they remain silent, either out of misplaced and wrongful "patriotism" or else out of fear- fear that they will forever be labeled unpatriotic, or a possible terrorist, or a dissident, or a malcontent. In a remarkable show of dishonesty, the media- bought out as it is- is fond of attempting to apply fringe political labels to anyone opposed to the ideals of one of our two major parties, even though those ideals are often indistinguishable.

You will remember how I mentioned this same facet in regards to race- that often politicians are so similar that the parties backing them have to force the public to compare their wealth, such that the public is able to perceive some difference between a millionaire and a slightly richer millionaire. The same is the case here with the ideals of the parties in all other respects, for the two major parties both support surveillance, torture ("enhanced interrogation"), censorship, busting up protests, the degradation of the constitution, and other moral evils. As such, they typically resort to wedge issues important to low-information voters, such as abortion, gay rights, or some other issue which they purposely take out of constitutional context, to weaken the latter and prop up the argument their party makes.

I have stated myself on occasion that the major difference between the two parties is not their views on government abuse but rather which aspects of life such abuse should be applied- the leftist parties in the western world typically wish to abuse people's wallets and destroy their right to defend themselves, to render them pacifistic and easily controlled. The right leaning parties of the west typically wish to control them on some religiously derived moral basis, especially in their sexual relationships or their ability to remain free of the constraints of religions they themselves are not members of. In the latter case we might say *"The right wing wants government to be small enough to fit in your bed."* And in the case of the left *The left wing wants government to be unseen enough to reach into your pocket and steal your wallet without you noticing."*

The same sort of bizarre situation played out in the Soviet Union as the single party system there led to a situation in which it was difficult to tell leaders apart- this leading to dictator after dictator (and later oligarch after oligarch to the present day) with similarly abusive views, who shielded themselves from criticism not by improving their own beliefs but rather by suppressing criticism and acting violently towards all dissent. Perhaps there are those who feel that at least the western governments haven't begun to execute dissidents, although some fear the day may not be long in coming where they will, since the people are increasingly disarmed, the police increasingly militarized, and the government increasingly eroding the first amendment.

In fact we might in a way say that the Soviets won the ideological struggle of the cold war simply because their mere existence forced our two major parties to combine, largely, on most issues- both parties share a pro-war stance (although candidates running for election may pretend to oppose war) and both parties share a love for the sort of police state tactics we once heavily decried when they were being employed by the Stasi of East Germany or within Russia towards anyone with disagreements with communism.

When we observe the fall of the Berlin Wall, we so often merely regard it as the fall of communism out of favor with the world at large- but I see in it something larger and less positive; namely that this barrier which had separated west from east was representative of the separation of the supposedly free west from the supposedly abusive east- and when this barrier fell, so too did the sort of ideological protection against those same abuses being used here, because in the absence of a powerful enemy, the enemy became the citizens at large within this nation itself and in all other western nations. Our representatives, who are almost all extremely wealthy and were born into the same, don't understand what it means to work for a living, and how difficult it is for someone who works to put food on the table to take the odd day off to go protest things- but then again it's not clear these representatives would care even if they hadn't been born into extravagant wealth.

So I say *Like the Nazis, the communists lost the physical war and collapsed, but the remnant of their ideologies, statist and totalitarian as they were, essentially won.* Again, as before, the same societal and political mistakes were made, and the government and culture of the western world right now, with its propaganda and surveillance, is no longer markedly different from the government and culture of East Germany.

One objection to this amongst well meaning but ignorant folks is to simply say "yes but it could be worse, we're still the most free." I argue that if you were to ask anyone around during this nations' founding if we qualified under our present state as free, liberated individuals, they would quickly say "No" and subsequently begin weeping that the nation they founded had been so wrongfully treated by its leadership.

The media is perhaps even more culpable than the government itself because of its lack of integrity and its new-found adoration for self-censorship and hand wringing. The days of the muckrakers are over, and the days of the media telling the public lie after lie in order to pacify them has begun. Media sites have even begun removing the ability of the public to comment on their internet based materials- they swear that this is due to abuse of the function but anyone with half a brain knows it's because people began hearing the truth- without the bias of the headline- in the comments, and these areas were becoming more important than the biased, usually woefully inaccurate stories themselves.

Much like Pravda or any other communist news network at the height of Soviet "glory" our own media has also transformed into a hideous mouthpiece for the government at large- and because they control virtually all media in some manner (including supposedly independent outlets) we hear mainly what they wish us to hear. The prospect of hearing real news doesn't get much better with foreign media, which again is just as controlled- and supposedly honest outlets which report the "truth" about our own representatives then spend a great deal of time defending their own leaders, most notably Russian media, which is perfectly willing to headhunt American politicians, only to fawn over their own Kremlin and pretend that their oligarchs never did anything wrong.

The "Us versus Them" mentality that has been thus crafted keeps most people in the dark when it comes to government abuse, and few if any of them realize that these abuses predominantly gained momentum after the second world war- for before the world wars the United States was largely pacifistic and had little standing military, low taxes, and was seen as a bastion of peace and progress because government was not only limited, but sometimes unable to enforce any wild demands they might have wished to state in the first place- it would have been difficult, for example, for some president in the mid 1800s to have enforced his will in the territories, where infrastructure was so rudimentary as to make large troop movements nearly impossible without severe attrition. Long gone are the happy days of limited government, it seems.

# IV: ISLAMOFASCISM WON AND PATRIOTS DID NOTHING

Islamofascism, which most notably (but not first) raised its ugly head on September 11th, 2001, also won its ideological crusade against the liberated western world, plunging us even further off the cliff into statism, interventionism, abuse, and censorship- everything ugly about a swollen government which no longer strictly represents the people and most often represents arms dealers, oil barons, the banking elite, and various corporate groups.

Osama Bin Laden, in all of his malevolence and evil power, must somewhere in Hell be looking up through the thin veil of the abyss and taking comfort in the fact that islamofascism has managed to render American (and western) society into the same self-censoring, paranoid wreck that was the islamic world of centuries ago. One specific problem the Arabian nations have had is that many aren't nations built on ethnicity, national consciousness, or even religion- they're chunks of Ottoman land carved into states by the British and French later on- the same is true of, say, Pakistan, which is also built up from several other states, such as Panjab, which got cobbled together after British dominance- colonization has largely had a negative impact on the world, true; but the tolerant left focuses solely on the racial motives involved and forsakes the pragmatic argument that, simply, colonial powers retreated, leaving behind infrastructure but little national consciousness to solidify these states, with the exception of a few such as India which is fairly stable.

When we say that the islamofascists won, it's clear we're not talking about technology or wealth or even kill count on a military basis- for in all of these measures, the western world has far outstripped all competition; indeed, because of population demographics I can here predict that we're not leaving, but entering, the American century, and that as even the most swiftly growing Asian states stagnate the west will continue churning along for another hundred or perhaps two hundred years, assuming no nuclear war wipes man out entirely.

Rather, it's the ideological struggle that they won; for islamofascism is marked especially by its own intolerance towards views outside of orthodox islamic philosophy, and marked also by its violent repression of such views that they find abhorrent- a nature they share with the same communists Osama himself once managed to destroy, back when he was getting funding and weapons from the United States under both Carter and Reagan. This facet of extremism is now shared mostly with our own government, and unfortunately by a proportion of our society, which is easily fooled and has swallowed the propaganda hook, line, and sinker.

Here I must submit that there is an intrinsic difference between islam and islamofascism- the two could not be further apart, and although some will think this to be naïve I will explain how I came to this conclusion- a conclusion I have shared with others largely to agreement.

When we consider a religion we must first consider its dogmatic system- that is, quite literally, what is said within its doctrines and pseudo-doctrines (in the case of christianity, thus, the bible and the semicanonized apocryphal and philosophical materials written by Luther, Aquinas, and others) and in the case of islam, the quran first and then the hadiths, of which there are a number- but the two most regarded hadiths which have the largest audience to accept their content are the *Sahih al Bukhari* and the *Sahih al Muslim.* When we consider the doctrines of islam, like those of most religions, we receive a mixed bag of violent materials and benevolent materials- and since it's clear that most western christians do not attack and behead people for disbelief, we have to assume the same doctrinal proclivity within islam- most muslims are uninvolved with such behaviors, although some may passively or philosophically accept them.

The second consideration of a religion is its current, modern-day use and interpretation by society and by its adherents where they are found, and here is where we see the disconnect between islam and christianity, as well as between mainstream muslims and the hardliners which terrorize civilians- for islamofascists and extremely zealous muslims largely support violence, and while others may passively accept it as *halal* or lawful behavior, I have met many, myself, who are *de facto* muslims living in the Arabian peninsula, who are pagans and atheists and dislike or are even hostile towards the religion itself.

## V: CONFUSED QUASI-RACISM

The current sad state of our Republic- which is as much a Republic at this point as Rome when the patrician classes chose imperialism over democratic will and began offering the position of permanent consul (emperor) to individuals thought deserving of such a title- is quite sad. With similar gusto, our society has forsaken the original founding notion that our legislative bodies were the primary arbiters of power and meant to do little more than represent the people's will, and has begun to see representatives as leaders (which was never meant to happen) and the rise of imperial presidents began almost as soon as the nation was born in the visage of the alien and sedition acts- which were hated, resulting in the subsequent election of Thomas Jefferson, who might be seen as one of our best presidents to date. This same sad situation exists in other forward-thinking, tolerant, supposedly enlightened cultures, where their legislators now act largely in an oligarchic manner with little or no regard to the nonsensical nature of some of the laws they pass, sometimes without themselves even fully reading or comprehending their content.

Society has begun to reflect this breakdown of order and logic, and is similarly confused, and this is no more evident than in the manner in which race and racism are regarded.

The first thing we must consider is the bizarre manner in which most people regard race- in most cases the concept is cultural and has little to do with biology or genetics to begin with. For example, in the United States, "Hispanic" was long a racial category, only recently being properly termed an ethnicity, one which in my own opinion matters little and is mostly arbitrary, perhaps concocted and retained for political purposes, so as to continue separating white Hispanics from those who are not "white", for fear of the same former group feeling connected to the latter. In parts of the world, the skin color matters not a bit, and it's the ability of an individual to prove "pure" ancestry- either purely white or black or anything else- that matters. In those cultures, one who has seven great grandparents who were purely of European stock and one great grandparent who was a native Mesoamerican, would be considered lower on the totem pole than a person with eight great grandparents who were all black slaves- this concept would seem odd to an American, who is used to seeing a racial hierarchy based upon the concept of "whites are at the top, and Asians and Jews kind of on the next tier, with everyone else gathered below."

In that strangely funny system, the quasi-populists of the right wing are no more or less confused and lacking in reason than the quasi-progressives of the left, all of whom take this system as king and merely derive different conclusions from it.

Regardless of which side of this arbitrary spectrum is interpreting this system, the differences are still important to them- the populist/nationalist sees it as a morally acceptable natural order and reacts violently when inequality is addressed or ameliorated, while the progressive/neoliberal sees it as a horrific monstrosity and wishes to destroy it- but the latter is no less intolerant, and typically blames white or higher-tier individuals as a collective; the same stereotyping and collectivist style of labels used by those populists who worry every time they see a black man.

In this manner, the left is guilty, clearly, of the same sins of the intolerant on the right- for the latter has simply focused their stereotyping, their anger and distrust, and their collectivist style of labeling people into categories, into a new system, in which "white" and "everyone else" are two separate entities- as such, they fully support discrimination, as long as it is aimed at the former. In an astonishing move, the further left individuals within that already far left group have now visibly begun to group Asians, who they see as privileged, in with the same anglo-saxon whites, further splitting American society apart.

That this system they have built is just as racist as that used by the populist has escaped the attention of most- and those few that notice and speak of it are almost always themselves populists, which means that most people will ignore them, giving them the title "racist" while largely ignoring the racism of the progressive.

In fact even the actions of progressive government have helped perpetuate racism- and here I submit that this was a conscious decision; from Nixon, who gobbled up the deep south by playing softball with the southern Democrats, to LBJ, who rammed civil rights legislation through with the express goal of gaining the support of the black voting population which had formerly been staunchly Republican.

The use of, for example, affirmative action, can only help further the racial divide of our society at large- not because "it disenfranchises whites!" or any other similar populist claim (whether some of those claims are valid or not) but simply because it creates an "us" and a "them" in the minds of all Americans- wherever such doctrines are used, you can be assured that those who perpetuate them do so not for pragmatic reasons but simply for dishonest ones- such was also the case with segregation, where it was repeatedly argued that it was a pragmatic solution that would prevent violent exchanges between groups who had been separated for their own good. The overall effect on society between segregation and affirmative action may be different, but the ultimate goal of those supporting both is the same, and the outcome (to divide the people into voting blocs) is equally similar.

Here we have to delve specifically into how government (bad government, that is) deliberately divides people into easily controlled, arbitrary groups for its own benefit- which is their crowning achievement.

## VI: STATISM IS THE DISEASE, OPPRESSION ITS SYMPTOM, AND ITS METHOD OF TRANSMISSION IS TO BREAK PEOPLE APART

It is exceedingly difficult for a government gone bad, suffering from the dry-rot of statism to actually enforce its totalitarian ideologies in a population acclimated to liberty, which is under little stress and in which most of the population lives a fulfilling life, or at least one in which their basic needs are fulfilled and easily acquired- here we can point out exactly how the three statist regimes I have already mentioned here actually came about to their existence- in two of these cases the society in question was largely one of peace and plenty before the rise of the statism in question, while in the case of the communists, it was predicated upon the willful destruction of a formerly advancing society, to its own detriment. Curiously, the same people who begin to tolerate statism invariably suffer the same fate- one of collapse both social and economic, for no nation can long exist under statism without being crippled.

In the case of Germany, the population was merely given an enemy (first, the Jews, and then other groups) to fixate upon, and then the Reichstag was burned- once war began it was easy to control most of the population which, scared as it was, was all the much more willing to fan the flames of racial nationalism and totalitarianism on its own, even without continual government goading. While millions of Germans, towards the end of the war, starved or suffered atrocity, the ones who had orchestrated the takeover lived in relative luxury.

Goering's strategy of burning the Reichstag and blaming it on communism worked- and the same thing, essentially, was done decades later at the Gulf of Tonkin- that in both cases the "conspiracy theorists" turned out to be objectively correct (in both cases the government had orchestrated its own casus belli) remains a hidden secret, and even though it is now admitted to be the case, many remain ignorant of reality.

In Germany at the time, the Nazis merely had to build upon the lingering fear and resentment people already harbored. Most of the time, a peace loving people will direct its anger in the proper direction, usually the government itself, which has been the arbiter of their own misery as the elite at the top absorbs more and more wealth, squeezing the life out of the lower, middle, and "upper" class (the last being a misnomer, for those making what to most seems a high income are still salaried workers whose productivity is largely stolen by the interventionists and statists themselves, with a small share being embezzled by corporations allowed to do so for the sake of a scapegoat.) The fact that Hitler endorsed the same model and was not a true socialist is an equally hidden aspect of the truth- because the left and right, in their bid to escape "being like Hitler" have both tried to foist his name off on the other side. In reality, he was just a statist and his economic views matter little.

In terms of Marxism the fear, paranoia, and splitting up of the population into arbitrary groups was still used, although here it was broken down not upon racial lines but economic ones- the same "upper" class I just mentioned was at first in control, leading an *intelligentsia* backed revolution against the Tsar and others, before swiftly being torn apart by Stalinist proletariat who declared that even this equally put-upon "upper" class was abusing the population as a whole.

So here, in a society which had already partially broken down and suffered economic as well as military setbacks, it sufficed not to blame someone on the outside for invading or destroying society, but rather to simply split people up according to the same hierarchical model the same communists decried. In a strange twist of fate, these equality-obsessed proletariat ignored the fact that many of the same urban intelligentsia they had just slaughtered had shared their same goal of reform.

Communism ultimately failed, but the statism remained- over the slow course of almost a century the people of Russia and areas controlled under Soviet rule grew accustomed to the graft, vice, and inefficiency of that same system, such that to this very day the communist party claims a substantial share of each vote.

Here we must see one of the most major evils of communism (which is invariably a totalitarian ideology requiring compulsory membership and a violent overthrow of existing systems as we have already seen time and time again) in that it creates the same misery which it requires to exist. In order to justify redistributionism, it is first necessary that there be a group of "haves" and one of "have nots"- and where these two groups are close enough together (or where the latter enjoys stability and some measure of dignity) it requires either violent overthrow or else continual propaganda to convince the latter that they would be better off under totalitarian, communist rule.

Unfortunately for the utopian communist, this hated system destroys more than it ever accomplishes and is impossible to implement in a vacuum without a state to function within, and as such requires statists to enforce it- military, police, propagandist media, and cruel and often lunacy-addled leaders to prop it up with misbegotten charisma.

Similar to this is islamofascism- for when it first was incarnated in its modern form it was encouraged directly by the western world itself as a solution to the same communists we just described. That it arose in areas which had been stable (and continues to do so) and was funded by the so-called enlightened "leadership" of the west is a matter of historical record.

Perhaps if those same leaders had known the problems it would spawn they would have found some other solution to the Soviet invasion of central Asia- perhaps it's naïve to think so, however, since the government and its many shadowy agencies largely acts in an oligarchic fashion and, in the modern sense, is still propping up jihadists- notably in Syria, where a formerly stable (but Russian-backed!) government has been at war with so-called "moderate" islamic rebels for some time now. This gave rise, as those moderate groups suffered severe attrition, to more hard-line rebels, who largely displaced them, having the same effect as the government's moves in Afghanistan in the late 1970s and into the Reagan era. This has happened as well in Libya, where a developed economy has collapsed entirely because the regime there was willfully displaced, and now refugees are streaming as of this writing, across into Europe by sea.

In fact, the government, statist and oligarchic as it has become, appears to have learned nothing, and unfortunately the population has again swallowed the bait- in the same way the Germans feared the communists and Jews, the American people and indeed the people of the entire west now fear a foreign statist system, and thus have no problem with home-grown statism in which the government has become a *de facto* singular person, an entity of sorts, with its own goal being nothing more than the enslavement of the population through the misuse of the people's own fear.

When these sorts of facts, true as they may be, are pointed out, the tendency among the government is to return to the same jaded, outdated allusion it always uses- the us and them mentality of a one party state which poses as one with two parties, with those same parties mostly united when it comes to surveillance, militarism, and interventionism- the United States has a plurality of political movements that oppose foreign adventurism and militarization but these parties have been marginalized because the two united, reigning parties have conspired dishonestly to deprive them of a platform in debates, and have gobbled up the media to preclude them from fairly competing; nonetheless we might see a glimmer of hope in the oft-straw manned libertarian party, or perhaps the constitutionalist movement. The fact that "fringe" candidates and absurdists have begun to make more logical sense than the things said by so-called mainstream candidates should have been a warning sign- a wake up call to the population that their government was in disarray, but most westerners look at politics as a sort of sports game, where two main sides duke it out, to the disclusion of any real competition for ideas.

In many parts of Europe there are more parties to choose from, but this is mostly an illusion of choice, for these parties, too, share more similarity than difference; one look at the tendencies of, say, the British conservatives and labour shows that they are mostly united in their views, and have conspired, equally, to marginalize smaller parties with better ideas such as UKIP- the same is true in France, where Front Nationale has equally been tarred and feathered with the "fringe" or "racist" label.

That the reigning parties are all corrupt, having held too much power for too long, and have conspired in this way, is common knowledge, but there remains the issue of how to break through to the average citizen and convince them they have been lied to. Unfortunately, statism has thrived in the west which once fought against it, partly because when things go wrong, whichever artificially concocted party is in power gets the blame, and people attempt to solve the problem by voting for the other party or parties- this invariably solves nothing, as whoever takes control continues the worst policies of the former and adds insult to injury by crafting ever more ridiculous ideas, which usually cost more than the nation can bear and solve nothing.

Statism itself is a disease- a cancer which once it takes hold tends to grow in scope until it destroys the host (a country or region or people) and then once collapse ensues, other statist movements invariably try to seize power- very rarely is this cycle broken by a true movement which cherishes liberty, and unfortunately even the most free society may eventually find itself stricken with this malady- the entire west, save for a few societies too rural and too remote to be affected- has been badly sickened by statist, totalitarian ideology in the last century, and the disease has progressed both here and abroad, in the eastern world which has malingered with it for even longer.

False patriotism is the worst symptom of all. A people, egged on by the same statists, can be made to delusionally support the same groups causing every problem, as long as those who call such groups out for what they are are labeled "unpatriotic"- in reality the groups being called this are the actual patriots- patriotism has been woefully misused as a label, and these days some believe it to mean "one who supports their government" or "one who conflates the will of the government and the nation as a whole as the same thing." This sort of unquestioning obeisance to "leaders" who do not represent the popular will, or even the popular good, is itself amongst the least patriotic virtues one can have.

It's not that people aren't aware that the government has become corrupt- they're fully aware of that fact- but the statists have managed to convince a large enough segment of the population that "the other party" or some other racial group or religion is responsible for their problems, in a manner only slightly less draconian and dishonest than the same strategy used by the Nazis or the communists in Soviet Russia- the goal has always been the same, to cling to power by splitting people into arbitrary groups which are then made to fight one another, so that they don't find it necessary to oppose a government which is "too big and scary" to fight. We see this echoed especially on the left, wherein former hippies who had once taken up ball bats and trash can lids to attack the DNC are now among the most supportive of public disarmament and the surveillance state. This is surprising, given they once considered themselves free and enlightened.

Cynicism is also one of the worse symptoms- people who truly know better than to support a government which has done little good and much harm both domestically and abroad have grown so cynical that they don't vote- including for third parties which could win with even a modest slice of the cynic vote- and not only this, they also don't protest, go to town meetings, or even complain about the government in public, because they feel all is hopeless and have stopped caring. These folks are by some considered lazy (*"where is your civic pride? Don't complain if you didn't vote!"*) although we can't blame them too much since the media and government have conspired to preclude most of these folks from even knowing that there are political movements and candidates who do not fit into the left-statist and right-statist dichotomy.

The greatest periods of prosperity in every part of the world have always coincided with periods of limited government, or even its absence, such as the at-best provisional legal and penal system existing in parts of these United States at the time of the homestead act- the same act that filled largely empty regions of land with settlers also saw millions moving into regions where there was little in the way of true government beyond the occasional military fort whose sole purpose was to defend trade routes from attack by Natives, or the town sheriff, who often was shot down if he was corrupt. We might here remark that violence, often thought to be common in those days, was actually fairly scarce because so many people carried firearms wherever they went.

# VII: THESE PROBLEMS ARE NOT HARD TO SOLVE BUT THE MEDIA AND GOVERNMENT MAKE THEM SO

Thankfully these problems here aren't particularly difficult to solve- statist regimes invariably collapse themselves anyways, but there are manners to prevent a collapse at all and to forcibly shove government back into the very small, very limited edifice it was meant to fill to begin with. Most people in the west are pacified or frightened of what they imagine to be a vast, powerful, almost omnipresent foe in the visage of a government which tracks their every movement and will execute them in the streets for dissent- which is partly true, but not really.

The first thing that must be done is for those who still value liberty to simply point out to others that the government is still made up of flesh and blood humans, who naturally compete with one another, thus preventing maximum efficiency- these agencies will stab one another in the back at the behest of their leaders to get a larger slice of the pie, and conspiracies revolving around some massive council of elites are unsubstantiated and probably crafted by the government itself to frighten people (here I submit that I am probably right when I claim that a large number of "conspiracy theories" are made by groups like the FBI and CIA specifically to distract those searching for the truth- 9/11, perhaps, is a good example of this.) These competing agencies, politicians, religious leaders, and generals, have always usurped one another, and this itself is often what predicates a statist collapse back into a quasi-anarchist period.

It must be said that I do not support anarchism nor does anyone with a working brain- this system is even worse and more unworkable than communism and is to be avoided whenever possible. Order is best maintained by a governing body which has been rabidly constrained to such a small level of power that its very existence is tenuous at any time and malleable, such that it can never, under any circumstances, begin to grant itself new powers- perhaps a *superconstitution* should eventually be considered, one which cannot be amended, and specifically prohibits the government from regulating speech, assembly, and weapons ownership, something unchanging that forms the national basis for western philosophy and isn't subject to court arguments or legislative changes- it would, of course, have to be a loose, generalized framework, lest the legislative body work its way around it as they have the constitution we use now.

Those who value liberty must also forsake cynicism- what party they vote for is ultimately less important than, at least temporarily, shunning the two major parties here or the major parties elsewhere in the western world- to pressure them is to force them to change, for political movements operate similar to the process of evolution, and when put under such pressures will change or else fall out of favor as the whigs did and disappear entirely. This is the second strategy which those who enjoy freedom may employ to revisit the concept of government and reform it where they are able.

Third, and perhaps most importantly of all, there must once and for all be a sort of standard for protest and organization that *must* at long last be stated here, that the disenfranchised ought to (if they wish to be successful) use to react to statism. So often, we see that a libertarian, or liberal, or constitutionalist, or other movement, falls flat because it immediately reacts to some ill real or imagined with violence. A few cars are burned, a few slogans chanted, and the police state moves right in, mops them up, and resistance withers. I will classify what I imagine to be the proper tiers here:

When an abuse occurs, the group involved in resistance ought first to petition, that is to make it known far and wide that an abuse has happened, and should attempt to build popular support for reform- if a government is able to be compelled to reform itself in a proper manner, no further action is necessary. (This, of course, is unlikely, although if the government itself is reformed or further constrained this may be easier in the future.)

If reform is not undertaken (and frequently lack of reform is defended by various cronies and lackeys, as well as by half the media- whichever half supports the party in power) then protest should be used. These protests should be strictly nonviolent, and if attacks occur they should be allowed to remain one sided, such that the government is shown to be the violent bully it so often is where such things are concerned.

If reform is still rendered impossible and the violence continues, there comes a point at which further civil disobedience (the breaking of petty laws to further media coverage and public support) becomes viable. As before, violence should not be undertaken.

If the issue is particularly important, then it is only at this point where all else has failed that the people have an inviolable right to stand their ground and not budge- nationwide strikes should be called for and any further violence by the state should be met with full resistance, and barricades should go up and the people refuse to stand down until their demands are met. If the state continues its violence, then by this time it is clear that protestors and citizens in general will have been killed by the frightened state, at which point the people should call upon any "fringe" or outcast government elements to back them and call for reform.

If at this final stage reform is still impossible, the people should consider themselves enslaved, and the government by virtue of its ignoring of the constitution to be null and void. The military itself should be compelled to stand with the people, acknowledging that the government has become illegitimate because it no longer represents either the public welfare or established constitutional code.

I take great heart in one fact, though, and this is where I differ from some within the libertarian ranks. I personally feel that the sense of pride instilled in the military would at the final stages override their loyalty to the government.

As such, although Milgram has shown that many would pull the trigger on a line of unarmed protestors, there would presumably be representatives and military brass that would defect as society breaks down, siding with the people over their so-called overlords who would necessarily have abandoned their own calling and would likely have already caused military families to be injured or killed. It would be at this point that the government would have destroyed its own legitimacy in the eyes of the troops, and the Marines in particular (in the United States) and various military branches in other locales, would I believe largely side with the people. A government, in the face of active resistance by branches of any armed service, would be unable to retain order and would break down in a manner similar to that seen towards the end of the Soviet Union when it became clear that high ranking military and political figures had chosen not to back what the communists declared to be a restoration of order. The people built their barricades, and they ended up backed by the president of Russia within the USSR as well as enough of the military to render the coup inoperable.

The final goal of the liberty-minded is simply to note that there is always hope- man has faced the hideous abuse of tyranny before, and every time it does the tyrant or tyrannical system is eventually done away with, often spontaneously, and as long as the people have organized properly, a further abusive system is less likely to replace the former.

# VIII: PEOPLE ARE BEGINNING TO WAKE UP, BUT THEY'RE STILL GROGGY AND NEED A COFFEE

Gandhi said *"First they ignore you, then they laugh at you, then they fight you, then you win."*

Regardless of what one thinks of Gandhi himself, the words here are still true. The media in the United States largely ignored libertarians and constitutionalists, as well as those advocating for the right to self defense- it ignored groups opposing the war in Iraq, it ignored critics of Joe McCarthy, it ignored those who pointed out the dangers of nuclear proliferation and the expansion of the cold war into Asia.

All through time the media, society, and governments at large have made the same mistake of attempting to ignore groups they dislike- the British media ignored UKIP until it began to expand rapidly, and now they have moved from the "laugh at you" stage to that of "then they fight you." The burgeoning libertarian movement in the United States is somewhere between these two stages, and I predict a bitter fight ahead, as the party attempts to reform election law and get itself into the debates and onto more ballots every cycle.

Those who support reform are almost always ridiculed until it becomes clear that the claims others once termed "fringe" or "loony" were correct. Those who said invading Iraq was a bad idea were termed unpatriotic hippies in 2003, but in 2007 they were regarded as having been correct. I am proud to count myself amongst them.

It is important at this juncture to simply once again point out to all of the partisans who might read this work that *there is very little actual difference between mainstream parties in almost any western nation.* This often overlooked objectively true fact is the basis for almost all of our misery, because the ideals held by the one party system each western "democracy" has, split into artificial parties with mostly the same views, do not work, and are almost always far more expansive, interventionist, and hawkish than benefits the general population.

Wars have been waged for just reasons in man's past- but we'd be hard pressed to find any modern examples of a war that was backed by any sense of justice- in fact in the modern age, we have to find examples of a pair of deeply impoverished third world nations fighting over who owns two thirds of some polluted river separating them to find a symmetric war that doesn't involve rebels or protestors or terrorists.

If the flame of the west is extinguished, mankind will fall into centuries of terror and intellectual darkness that will make the worst times of the medieval era look like playtime with tea and stuffed animals- for in the modern age we have nuclear plants that could melt down and release particles of radioactive elements if not tended to, should order break down (some have claimed modern plants don't melt down- I'd point out that most existing plants use the older designs which do.)

We are also reliant upon genetically modified food sources which require extensive chemical use. We're reliant upon vaccines which have marginalized disease without destroying it- even polio has made a comeback.

The modern man would be barely able to survive, let alone expand, in a world where some of his modern comforts and technology become impossible due to social breakdown, and perhaps the easiest way to see this breakdown occur would be to let the statists have free reign to abuse our economy into inefficiency or our society into slave status. A free people work harder, think smarter, and function at a greater maximum of comfort and peace, and should totalitarianism take hold in the west, this peace will not be retained. Last I would mention nuclear weapons- for what happens to them, should hawkish statists with no common sense acquire the nuclear codes? This world would end in a blistering inferno, and there would be very little left to salvage.

So let every man stand on his feet and declare himself free, and let him act as though this is true, not merely obeying some far-off and illegitimate superior, but let him consider himself alone his superior and the government his inferior- for that is what government is actually meant to be, not the leader but the led.

*"Those who surrender freedom for security will not have, nor do they deserve, either one."* -Benjamin Franklin